Color
Outside Lines

Color Outside Lines is a self-instruction to disregard instructions. The collection of poems comes out of attempts to understand tolerance and awareness in society, sprinkled with some enquiry and some disregard for prejudiced notions. The poems unite to discuss topics ranging from duty-faith to expression and inquiry that are often viewed as purely right-wing or liberal issues but hide subtleties that often evade a casual observer. The refrain encourages the reader to opinionate for one's own self while carefully guarding against distracting and enticing demagogic forces.

It may not always be possible to convey all facts, perspectives and versions of a topic "in 140 characters or less" or "in 1 minute clickbait videos" or "in three stanzas of rhyme." These poems, borne out of thought provoking discussions over umpteen cups of *chai* and coffee, aspire to serve as kindling for further sharing of ideas and perspectives.

The poems propose that the pursuit of informed opinions about nuanced topics should be the wind of our sails as well as the compass of our times. In that vein, *Color Outside Lines* is dedicated to the impassioned exchange of views joined by threads of reason that leads to the making and changing of opinions and minds.

Color Outside Lines

Purujeet Parida

HAR-ANAND
PUBLICATIONS PVT LTD

Published by Ashok Gosain and Ashish Gosain for:
HAR-ANAND PUBLICATIONS PVT LTD
E-49/3, Okhla Industrial Area, Phase-II, New Delhi-110020
Tel: 41603490
E-mail: info@haranandbooks.com/haranand@rediffmail.com
Shop online at: www.haranandbooks.com
Like us on www.facebook.com/haranandbooks

Printed in India at Arya Printers

Contents

Paperboats after it Rains

A flame burns bright in every fire,
that draws a moth to its bane.
With a flutter and a spark, a death march,
if in vain, what remains turns insane.
Why is it so that moths must die?

So more may come and be gone.
Why is it that the flame did lie?
Does it matter? When needed, it shone.

In the dark, the glowering sphere,
flickers at darkness- a losing game.
A gust of wind may kill the flame.
A drop of rain can do the same.
It lives on borrowed time here.

Hours after the heavens opened first,
with a tattoo of drips from leaf tips,
comes a patter of small feet and chirps.
Rustle of paper, lighting of herbs,
a prayer, before the shrine and shrubs.
A marriage of kings, a child's game,
plays out to merry nonsense refrain.
By the tree over the clear running stream,
wed royal dolls, with incense and flame.
Happy eyes, in fantasy, gleam.
Solemn hands fold, other are joined,
Without words, enough is said.
Thin candles lit, fixed up straight,
In the paperboats, they had made.
While the paperboats float away in the stream,
the fire, with no moths around, is aflame.

The children part, those of the after-it-rained,
witnesses to a suburbian momentary eden.
Year later they met, the childhood friends.
By the street where once the stream ran.
But it was not the same.

One couldn't for example,
make Paperboats after it rains.
And no moths were dying
from the electric flame.
No bird to be found downtown.
Not eyes, cameras lifted at the rain.
Some turns good, some rots bad:
Nothing, ever, stays same.

Haiku Harakiri

The Man harvests, chops off corn.
For Food and Riches,
eats, sells, sows again.

In the dry summer,
Happily the children play,
parents yearn for rain.

Worry seeps through cracks,
Rainclouds invisible yet.
Weatherman is God.

Birds fly to sunset,
Scent of rain tantalises.
Earth smells sweet from far.
Prepare come sunrise,
To till the land, start again,
For Food and Riches.

For Family when,
Seeing in midwinter chill,
Filled bellies bring smiles.

A Posterboy for Hell

From birth till death, we're met with these –
YinYang like dichotomous analogies.
For the sake of heaven, Oh so many of these –
Incredibly flabbergasting Divine stories.

Indubitable men and women lie, lying to get by

and others incensed, should even one disagrees.
Oh Lord! What a game we invent ourselves;

Where the rules are ours, sour? sure sire;
Where Divinity could not be born elsewhere;
Where popular rule can also be a blot;
Where tyranny under the sun mayn't miss a spot;
Women hide, huddle, hushed? sure, why not?

We play it everywhere,
in our homes and outside.
We bring children into the fold,
by obedience abide.
We may loot or lose our fortunes in the telling
of omnipotent God and after-life tales
What a game we indulge in,
with faith and respect
In faith, believing, if everything else fails.

God helps those who help themselves.
Oh, What a Game we have invented for us!
Where we run on like enslaved white rats,
to human-determined destinies, just not ours,
for the supposedly one and only Divine,
just not theirs,
Wondering, waveringly unsure of Godliness
Seeing through scripture, blind to Godlessness

Like to the guards, the chiming of hanging tower,
Duty and honour for some, for others,
Death Knell.
Unthinking, Uncaring,
Understandably blessed, we are
Supermodels for heaven,
Tortured Posterboys for hell.

What a game we have invented,
Our children and theirs must play.
Going from Charity to holy massacre,
for good or worse –
The Game is here to stay!

Offensive Defense of Faith

It may be offensive that some take no offence,
when a depiction of peace
turns death sentence.
It may not be offensive to some, but not me.

It may be offensive that some take offence
when divinity transcends understanding
where faith begets confidence,

Dogma brings peace
where unseen mysteries abound,
sanguine as the seas
where conviction gives way
to jubilant ignorance

It may be offensive that some take offence
when a well meaning prayer turns sour
It may be offensive to some, but not me.
I am too scared for my life
to worry about afterlife.

I am too scared of men to worry about time.
I am too scared of offensive defenders of faith.

Offended and scared to be openly
speaking my mind,
and rightly so, as I'm honestly advised.
Still, In that I might have lost already
to the voices that seek to silence me
Still, I cannot but revolt within
against self-censorship in cowardice.

Maybe what is needed is not more Courage
from those who are ready to die
Maybe what is needed is more Shame
from those who are ready to kill

Moonlit Hike

The flurry of daytime activity dies
with dusk, then insect cries fill in.
Some creatures hunted, others hunting
with darkness piercing eyes, "Look out,
for shining orbs!" says the scout
as by the cliffside, we are climbing.

Wispy clouds wave whimsical shapes
and yet, fractured, moonlight escapes
casting a cool sheen over the rocks
the shrubs, by the steep steps.

We are climbing, pulling up, straining
Unsure of the goal, yet silently striving
Wordsworth strolling through daffodil fields
watching country women sing folk songs
Barely enough now, One now needs
to step beyond where one thinks one belongs
Is it progress, hubris or natural curiosity?
Are we seeking what we're supposed to need?

Train of trudging trekkers pause
Round a particularly scenic turn.
By a balancing rock, cactus forest
with a black and white valley
in front. Cameras click away.

All photos turn Stern. However,
As clouds clear, the moon shines through.
All trekkers, still silent, feel a bond renewed.

No one speaks, we all agree to move on
The peak is more visible, not closer yet.
Only the breaths are getting shorter,

like the steps,
Not the desire or drive, to climb on,
with the rest.

The wily red fox sulks at the hunched forms
invading its turf, it waits on us,
fur shimmering
and eyes gleaming at us. Backdrop of stars
show a retreating form by the gnarled tree
We were allowed to pass, not all were aware.

And so we reached the "CliffHead"
from where we could see the sea

In a few hours, when the moon sets
it would light up a line on the sea
Now, To find a patch of soggy grass
sit and enjoy uniquely personal
Fruits of labour – Worth the hike!

Deserving Destiny by Chancing upon Chances

Mice and men live a lie together,
crowding like birds of a feather;
dreams they weave,forgetting bother,
in this Nation of light,
where right comes from might,
where hope wins in vain o'er night,
where one sapling sucks up the moisture,

killing seeds sowing hope in fracture,
with thousands such saplings in sight;
yet future seems but flickering light.

To the Wise, the chaos is teetering,
others surmise, change is dithering,
Like candle flame, position and name;
unsteady in the face of bickering.
It's all a game, no one has shame,
showing up and cursing all who came,
grandson of queen, son of no king.
The bricks that miss make the country lame.

It's time for the soul, not solace
before challenges that we face.
Hankering over hangovers of history;
it's possible, our futures we deface,
it's possible we are all not wise,
it's possible to criticize, not debase,
Can we rise up and smell the lies?
Can we conquer the stench of Complacency?
Can we lay to rest, this vice?

For the rising sun ahead, is no birthright,
To be worthy is to pay the price.
It's only right to fight,
your way towards canopy;
It's a Jungle on the blue planet,
No room for complacency.

One Day

Since I was a child,
the "night follows day" refrain
seeks to pause my life;
But handy rotating earth,
such a no-nonsense timekeeper.
No early riser ever

made a good time of the night, except
One day means nothing
more or less than the night.

The Present, nothing less or more
Unique, Transient, Full of choice
What changes when change is constant,
Doesn't it all stay the same, when change is constant?

Doesn't a newspaper headline One day
take you back to the 90's?
Doesn't some parody of ad-jingles One day,
run springles down your spine?
Doesn't it feel desolate One day when tactics, leaders,
supporters, news, weapons and fighters,
have all changed, but crises remain constant?
Doesn't that same MJ song scream Revelation! One day;
When criminals openly, criminally and smoothly thrust,
themselves in our faces and on seats of power and trust.
What Really changes when change is constant?

A different set of people to get packed
into suburban trains;
A different set of simpletons to get conned
into illusions;
A different set of oppressors to declare
themselves rulers;

A different set of businesses for corporate emperors.
A different set of people to live an oblivious life,
complaining
that everything is changing so fast,
when nothing really is.

One day may not solve a crime
One day will take to start solving
One day may not make a national reprieve
One day will take to start thinking
One day will you have?
One day when We All need it?

One day when you don't stand for spitters,
cheaters, criminal overlords, political underpins
plotless movies, hapless babas, touts and crooks
in general, that One day counts,
every time, every where.

One day you will look up and stand up
Won't you? One day will you vote Right, not rightest?
For example, One day will you sigh and accept,
it's really "None of the Above."
And that is when something might Finally Change!

Following Voices

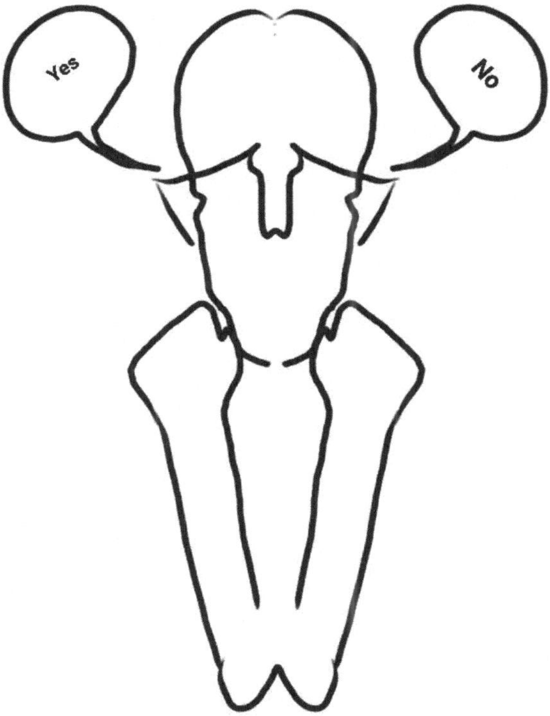

When the voices seem to follow you
But you are sure that you know the truth
Following the voices that sing the song
Of a beautiful bliss, awaiting beyond
Just then you're proved wrong
Pushed back, Plans Undone

You can swallow some pills,
Or do anything that kills.
You can jump in the sea,
Or onshore, Lie and Breathe.
Fire Up your Karma, or Inwardly Seethe,
Or Give up and turn numb inside,
Won't you never give up without a fight?

Don't tell me I didn't warn you,
Not to follow the voices that follow you,
If what they warn, turns out to be true;
If what they stand for, comes out for you;
If silently screams, turn everything Blue,
Color me red, a nonentity besides.
But conscience gnawing at your sides.

You can jump in the sea
Or onshore, Lie and Breathe
Fire Up your Karma, or Inwardly Seethe
Or Give up and turn numb inside
Won't you never give up without a fight?

Open shut eyes, See the beauty of Earth,
through telescopes, not rangefinders.
For Crosshairs make the world cry,
one needless death at a time.
Blasphemy! should need no killing.

By only killing, Have you sinned?
Self Inquiry! Not Inquisition!
Blasphemy! Oh by definition!

You can jump in the sea
Or onshore, Lie and Breathe
Fire Up your Karma, or Inwardly Seethe
Or Give up and turn numb inside
Won't you never give up without a fight?

Wandering the Countryside

Just wandering the countryside
In search of stranger firesides
Is it foolish, Is it futile?

This walk without a direction,
This search for nothing at all.
Nothing in particular, everything in the world

The driftwood finding pristine shore
but in it, finding everything to desire

Everything is by the wayside.
of the roads that cannot be denied.
Everything transient, in the mind.
All thoughts from memory, pried.

Everything stays, while moving on,
Now is fleeting, Now is past.
No matter the rose by the bush,
Nor the cuckoo's song,
Nothing more spectacular
than faces, we all put on –

In lullaby and mourning cry,
In hushed tales of a spy,
In chattered myths of spouses,
In transparent lies of children,
In flung curses of misled righteous,
In whispered wondrous words of love

By the moonlight, in the forest
where the white flowers often bloom.
Hands clasped, wander on
Measured by none.
Followed by none.

Meanderingly carry on,
like so many a wordless song.

Just wandering the countryside
In search of stranger firesides
Is it foolish, Is it but futile?
To find everything in search of nothing
What works? Innermost thoughts or stimuli?

Crisis – Beware

Crisis of faith, crisis of love,
tapping, pulling on strings,
like the god who sits above.
Wondering if all
the time in the world,

is not a moment to be wasted.
Past that craves to be bested,
is not that dark, your soul
is not just your living hole.
By effort, time is rested,
by tomorrow, today, crested.

A prime-mover in your mind,
is facing this crisis of faith.
Interlacing, penetrating
through the whims of unseen fate.

Crisis of faith, crisis of love,
tapping, pulling on strings
like the god who sits above.

Elite beings from surreal dreams,
stay, stay stay with me;
Forever stay or go away.
Where you are and there you will be,
old and naked, for the world to see.
For what time is next, what follows death
pales 'fore lifetime, at least what's left.

Crisis of faith, crisis of love
tapping, pulling on strings
is no god who sits above.

Each one get your act together,
now now now or never.
Your will is loose strings,
just for you, not another.
Tragedy is bound by rings,
put out and see what brings.
Your life, life, life or death –
’tis no time to cry or idly fret

Crisis of faith, crisis of love,
pulling away on social strings,
Prejudice, ignorance sprouting seeds;
Hatred, mistrust spreading disease;
We must close the scores, open minds.

System and tyranny, incorrigible shit
We must do our bit, to clean it
Crisis of faith musn’t be crisis of living
ISIS of today mustn’t paralyse the levant
We must stop it, not ignore it

’tis Between you and God who sits above
Who ends this crisis of faith and love
But if our children and theirs, must suffer
will any loving God forgive who forgets love?

Bird on a Wire

A Ball of feathers sitting on a taut string,
scanning eyes gently swaying with the wind.
Quick to swoop on unsuspecting worm,
Who knew too late, what fate will bring.

"What do you see, up here like me?"
Said the bored wire to the bird.
It screeched before tilting its head,

shocked, not one to leave it unsaid,
"You speak? Or just a voice in my head?!"

Humming its laugh, the wire continued –
"I do enjoy watching the daily feud,
the one each one does have down there.
I watch from above, how they fare."

Nodding agreement, the bird replied –
" If I cared, I would have sighed,
how they run from fold to fold.
The in-betweens of stories untold."

"Sing me a song!", said wire to bird.
"A sweet melody to pass the time,
I care not for words or rhyme"
People rushed below, no one heard
the soulful music of the songbird.
With tears, no eyes were blurred.
In empty hearts, no feelings stirred.

Come dusk, with the light, the bird has gone
Left hanging, the wire hums alone
For rushing, teeming busy humans
The long day is not yet done
The long day is not yet done

Forest of Matchsticks

I burned down a forest last night.
Ash and smoke everywhere,
I was choking, but I didn't care.
I would light it just for kicks.
The bloody forest of matchsticks.

Smoke stands still in the air,
soiled by the sodden affair,
Ukraine was grabbed by the pair
and children burned, as mothers watched;

cities were torched, as countries delayed,
a solution that was quick and fair.
Too many dying, too few to care.

Like the tinderbox 2.0,
you need a fire? Light it so,
it's only easy when you know,
once burned, forever stays so.

So why delay? why not say –
"Enough. Now it must give way."
Isn't it already too late to pray?
By actions, nations, must fears, allay.

The forest of problems ignored, grows,
the solution is slowly but surely lost.
So I grasped it where it mostly pricks,
I could, but did not do it for kicks.
Though I burned it anyway,
the whole forest of matchsticks.

I burned down a forest last night.
Ash and smoke everywhere,
I was choking, but I didn't care.
I would light it just for kicks.
The bloody forest of matchsticks.

But "Today", no army can fix,
nor any meeting of G-6.
War begets war, as true as time ticks
Peace is never made from hurled bricks
Power will just not break the jinx,
How will it burn then? - I wonder.
This bloody forest of matchsticks.

Mickey on the Moon

What shines dim and cold, like white gold,
on these farms and fields of countryside?
What gives the blue sheen, like aquamarine,
to shadows and silhouettes in my mind.

What do we do? What have I done?
Has the story ended? Has it begun?
By the glimmering river, under the Banyan
Opening up to a new dimension

It's so cold, the still moonlight
It's so bright, but I miss the sun!
What pricks at the edge of my vision?
What moves, but stays out of sight?
What do we do? What have I done?
Has anything changed in a minute?

"Sit tight", a voice in fright.
Did he say it? Did I hear it?
whispering trees, shimmering current
under a rabbit tattooed moon's light

But what is it? What is that face?
round eyes and mousy nose?
scoffing laughter rings about.
Does he see it? Did he hear it?
Blink and it is gone, too soon.
"Was that Mickey on the moon?
Did he say it? Did I hear it?

The riverbed saw two running figures
one picks the other, who stumbles
from time to time, they point at the moon
and howl like convicts in shackles
The clouds come swooping from the south
As Mickey on the moon scans about

Blackness sneaks up on blue sheen
A stupor settles over the scene
No ripples nor splashes on the river
Swiftly the clouds hide the moon
As demonic eyes search, in vain
Two screaming shadows nowhere to be seen.

Stalactite

Rushing heavens have no pull,
on underground caves of lime.
In darkness, in water, thrives life,
sightless, but with infinite time.

Drip, drip, drips the water,
having drunk mineral slime.
Drip, drip on the boulder,
Tireless is nature's Rhyme.

From heights, through cracks
from streams, pools and rain
from The Sun's tireless toils
or the apathetic human's spoils
Nothing above ground may remain same

Drip, drip, drips the water,
having drunk mineral slime,
Drip, drip from the boulder,
Timeless is nature's Rhyme.

Ballads sung, stories forgotten;
Empire's rise, Rome's fall;
Death and life, a roulette's spin;
Virtue or sin, may equally win;
Nothing of human concern may stall.

Drip, drip, drips the water,
having drunk mineral slime,
Drip, drip from the boulder,
Tireless, Timeless nature's Rhyme.

Tower of lime, broad of base
grows steadily and slowly
Rising, as if by magic, in space
To friendly inching cone above
as water turns architect with grace.

Each the other, ceaselessly seeks.
Crest meets trough, in geological blinks.
What remains of Stalagmite, if the water is spent?
What if one day the Stalactite, is broken or bent?

Both live and grow, as long as waters flow.
Alone, they stand, until they die hollow.
What happens in hollow lime caves on earth,
is Timeless loneliness or Tireless life.
Pillar of strength or spikes in spite,
A love story of Stalactite and Stalagmite.

Whole Again

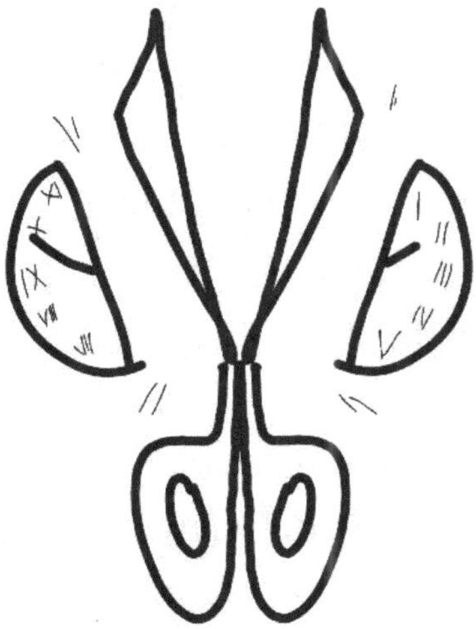

A nervous wielder of the shear is here to erase,
without judgement, the condemned from sight.
Those whose folly it was to be loyal;
Those whose folly it was to be born;
Those whose folly it was to be dead
on the wrong side.

What right slicing of time would be right sized
in rightfully citing the righteous glory of victory
wrought by the Right against the Wrong?

The wrong lives of the wrong who wronged
the strong who now know of the wrongdoing
and wrong the once strong who wronged
their own right side.

Who can see the men of the blind shear?
Those who wielded it are no longer here.
Those who wield it strut not its power.
Those who know its yield are not yet here.
Yet the shear shears sheer lines of fear
into minds that are easy to steer
and drift onto either side.

Now we have shears in our minds
that neatly collage our world view for us,
helped by declarations of love and war
nudged by activism of loss and despair
nurtured by cynicism of thankless tomorrows.

Now we could have those shears in our minds
to neatly trim the deadwood from our trunks
to puff up the crown for tiny sparrows to nest in
to make a garden of earthly perspectives
to sport a hobby of peace grabbing

Or we could have those shears in our minds
cut out the color, shred the happiness,

relieve reality of its serenity
reduce heterogeneity to heredity
revise reproductions of history.

If these shears are to know the mind without fears
If these blades are to bear only upon mean dividers
If these craftsmen of tomorrow are to rehearse
their version of yesterday in today's verse
we would have hope on both sides,
else on none.

Those Hills have Flowers

What does a man do, when he's lost his way?
What hope does he have, who will be his savior?
Won't there be a miracle to get him out of his hole?
If something does happen, could it not just as easily be,
A mishap?
If a sigh does escape, could it be brought back,
with a snap?
What use in waiting for the bus that may never come?

What signs must one see to forget one's way home?
What use is sense, of direction and empathy?
When, lost in woods, instead of wonder, you pander…

To whims of fast diminishing courage and false gaity,
To pulls of ancient hormones and basal instincts,
to make noise and laugh and even maybe sing,
Trying to shoo away darkness and find hope,
somewhere.

Somewhere is where one must go to find oneselves, they say.
Somewhere else though, always somewhere else.

What is so wrong with the here, the now?
What is so bad about a row of mute trees and silent ghosts?
What is so scary about a host of thieving clouds
scheming past a nonchalant moon?
When, hallway up the slope, you think you hear howling,
from in front, and from behind you. All around.
What is so wrong in prayer? In praying for a miracle?
What would you do just then, if the ground goes missing?
If suddenly you find the sky swooring for joy, at your misfortune,

Won't you find yourself in the deepest of troubles?
What could a man do, stuck in a hole on the side of a mountain?
With wolverines and jackals on the hunt for his hide,
With sniggering ghosts sitting with swag on trees,
With nothing but a glimmer of hope,
in the form of actual glimmer through the trees,
to calm your defeated nerves and nihilist heart.
What could a man do but sigh, just when he oughtn't to have?
When the light of a swerving car quits being his morning sun,
When clawing at the walls he finds, no purchase, only sellouts,
What could a man do, but dig his own way out of the hole?

When rescue dogs find the pit next morning,
they would not know what they see, but they would smell.
They would smell the nervousness of a man who knows,
He must Jump to Fly, but he knows how to do neither.
So he must put his head down and dig his way over.
Over the crest he could not see, not because it was too high
but because it was nighttime and he could not see in the dark.

If the dogs had arrived hours early, with the sun,
They would have seen a blackened, bleeding, smiling man;
Emerge from the other side of the hill of wolverines and jackals.
For, What can a man do but Smile when he sees
in the first light of a summer sun,
clearly, from afar, the colors that beg for attention.
Clearly, his tunnel, the darkness and company of moles,
had turned mishap to miracle and made his last night expire.
What does a man do now that he is free?
From his long night of troubles,
From his need for salvation,
From his need to call any place home,
What can a man really do?
He gets up, dusts himself and sets forth.
Why, on to the next hill to continue his toil?
Because that hill has flowers, and
as his own savior, he deserves one.

Light behind the Clouds

Silver linings are scarce consolation
for the absence of rainbows.
But they give all indication
that the sun still shines.

One winter they moved to the country.
Idyllic cottage by the shed and barn
to bring order into chaos

and disarray of city-life.
That winter their cow died before their horse
and their dog met with an accident
The kids flunked their first class and
their hens kept running out
into the snow to be frozen and
their solar power reserves and patience
was running dangerously low.

By summer they were fighting over
who threw paper in the toilet bowl.
Hungry kids and an angry dog come as a lot.
Every summer day is twice the winter lot
When their dog died they cried together
for the first time after moving.
All was quiet for a while as everyone figured.
Victories not worth it are also hard fought.

As trees soon to be nude wear colors
stealthy showers spoil half the standing crops
swift cold wind lashes at windows
and bears start to rummage up dustbins
to avoid starving in their slumber.
But from the children's room comes laughter.
A bottle filled freshly with firefly flutter.
A necklace of dried wild flowers for mother.
A cow-horn mug etched with love for father.

That winter the chill was harsher
but they were ready with their learnings
with silver linings on their blankets and in their minds
that summer was coming.
Every summer day is twice the winter lot.
It was better than nothing.
Fishing on the lake, with visiting campers,
learning to play the organ in tune with the guitars,
listening to stories from another planet,
with concrete forests and skyscraping loneliness.
The smell of barbeque, fish and pork
and wine from grapes that will escape the frost.
Long summer evenings were coming
because dismal today is silver lining
to the mesmerizing sunsets that are coming.
Here, now, that is something.
Something they did not know was missing.

Sticks and Stones

A tree fell in a forest silently perhaps.
No one saw it fall and time elapsed.
Green to grey, supple to stiff, it turned,
until an ape stumbled upon it and learned,
lightening lights up dried, dead trees,
it burns and kills, pursues and frees.

A branch burning behind the bush, he found.
A family of squirrels charred to death.
He poked and picked off the meat.
Dragging burning branches through the forest.
He brought accidentally cooked food that night.

From that dead tree, one made a club and
bashed the head of the excited ape man.
Another picked off a stiff arm, and burned it
and made a bone spear to spike things with.

But once the fire died, the night rolled in.
Once the blood first stopped flowing
Once the armed and alive sing
Once man gained a pointy sting
For the stick, there was NO Stopping.

Then maybe stones struck to smash shells
or maybe hurled to crack heads
maybe sparked and lit dried leaves
maybe someone noticed it.
maybe repeated it, like the monkeys
they once were.

By cooking, one half made sure,
All the meat doesn't go to the hunter,

By chipping rock, a once blunt spear,
became a human life-eater.

Was it so surprising, that we melted rocks
to make pointed sticks to kill with?
Is it so surprising that the family was
to be saved by killing other filth?

Yes we did stick stones on sticks to
plough and farm and herd with.
But the power and new found divinity,
rested and maybe still does, with prosperity.

Prosper with arms, thrive on others' behalf;
Prosper with Laws, spoken on others' behalf;
Prosper with conquest, thrust on others' land;
Prosper with belonging, snatched from others.

Slowly as an egg becomes a moth,
A stick to be missile, sought
A stone by being a bomb, wrought
A Hiroshima and a Cuban crisis
Worship of sticks and stones made
A toothless world against Isis

Sticks and stones, have broken bones,
and cultures, who among us atones?

Sticks and stones, have enslaved us,
illusion of safety, who among us sees?
Sticks and stones, have silenced us,
against jingoist pseudo secularist foes,
Sticks and stones in hand, we have,
forgotten to hold hands,
forgotten to share lands,
Forgotten that it all ends,
as sticky mush with stabbed futures.

The Praying Atheist

Every day the man rises to Azaan,
and steps out to work by the time of aarti.
He passes by the marigold garlands
to stop by the smiling shoeshine boy.
He does not tip but he hands him his money.
He waits while someone in more of a hurry
forgets to say sorry after cutting in the queue

His clock starts ticking with coffee,
listening to excited colleagues
prattling on about baby showers and baba parties.
He sees the fasting man quietly leave before
others share round Prasad in round containers
and eat round veg pizzas on a different round table.
He applies for leave on an obscure holiday
and steps out for fresh air every once in a while.

The tea-seller hands him his change;
The snacks-seller shakes his head at the note;
The blind beggar at the corner is putting up his stall
and just when the chai is just hot enough
it starts to rain and the blue tarpaulin is rolled out.
Swiftly the drizzle becomes downpour;
He hears the stranded pray and curse and
shout over the rain, into phones and faces,
huddled in formals, avoiding the beggar's corner.

He waits for time to tick closer to the close,
worries about beggars and suiciding farmers on the
auto;
stands next to a woman advocating sexism on the train;
sits next to a man advocating dictatorship on the bus;
walks by a couple discreetly nestled behind one bush,
and gives a wide berth to a man peeing on another bush,
and smiles at the non-responsive watchman looking

at a family lighting floating candles for a birthday.
He pauses and makes a wish before he asks himself,
"If anyone is truly listening, Why will he listen to me?"

He shrugs, and pays no more attention to it
than he does to the poison and the nectar
that is peddled every day in the name of the listener.
If nobody is listening, no prayer is required.
Else, questioning his existence is his prayer

Tic Tac Toe History

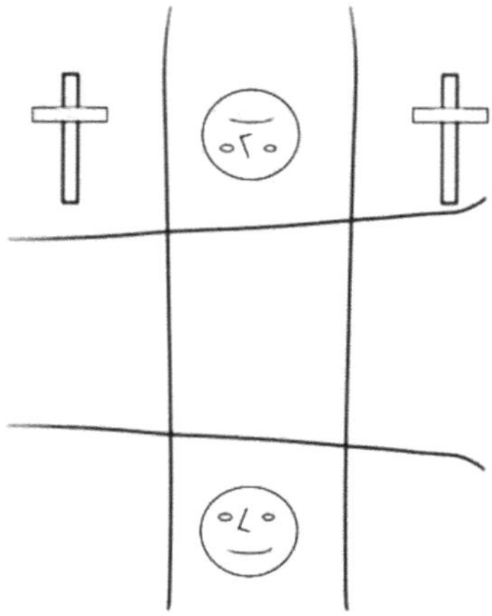

Come let's play a game, let's say tic-tac-toe.
Pick a pen and a spot, Cross or loop it so.

Show me a war with a winner.
with a circle, make it clear
and I'll show you the sufferer,
same the peaceful as the marauder.

Show me a land with traditional discrimination
I'll show you people with muzzled mouths, minds, lives

Show me a much-loved ruler with unparalleled glory
I'll show you what a curious exception she makes

Show me a system of obedience and peace
I'll show you how with a flourish,
with a hoop and/or a cross,

Change the chorus, shift the rhetoric,
selective reads and out of context, serves,
you can draw attention where it pleases
and where it hurts, make it go away.
Make it what you like, do as you may.

Come let's play a game, let's say tic-tac-toe.
Pick a pen and a spot, Cross or loop it so.

If I win with crosses, they become loops.
If I win with loops, they remain the same.
What we cross is and stays forgotten.
Or what is the point of this game?

Time, the great healer, can repair wounds,
 then again, no one can reverse amputation.
History, the greatest story, can be learned from,
 then again, no one can refute its repetition.

Perspective, of only the winners, can guide the future,
then again, any other perspective is long gone.

Once we see what we saw, what is seen is gone.
Think of the millennia past, how much of it is known?
Thank Ra! For the history sleuths who must dig and dive,
or no one who know or care to know, what was known.

Would we know of the teachings of Zarathustra,
 without unexpected mercies?
Would we know of ruins of Ancient Harappa,
 without its lackluster modernity?
Would we know of Devanampriya Ashoka
 without traitorous Bengali nobility?

If you know you know, or you know you have to,
or not and that's really all there is to it.

Come let's play a game, let's say tic-tac-toe.
Pick a pen and a spot, Cross or loop it so.

There's this thing I know that I'd rather you not know about,
So I can swindle this drink away from you,
There's this thing your grandfather pointed out to you,
so you won't take it back, what if I touch you?
Careful! One moment before you make a mark, think.
A mark made, is known and by it, are you – a cross or a ring?

Careful but fast, life is passing by with every blink.
Participate or be forever alone at the brink.

Oh it's too much you say?
Too much minority love in Political Parties?
But you were born into a culture under attack.
Too much murder and mayhem in the paper?
But you never really read it anymore.
Too much random chaos and promotions on twitter?
But you were only ever on it for the jokes.
Too much shouting without points on TV? Or
Too much whining and dining on Instagram? Or
Too much meetings over buffet lunches? Or
Too many Laws and circulars to quick read? Or
Too many opinions you need to have? Or
Too many decisions you have to take? Or
Too many children starved to death? Or
Too many lives lost in jail? Or
Too many sons dead in Militancy? Or
Too many innocents shot at protests? Or
Too many Tribal villages burnt at high stakes? Or
Too many liberals in alive and active state? Or
Have you lost your pen, paper and mind too?

I only asked you to play Tic-Tac-Toe then.
It was not to be played all the time.
You don't need an opinion this badly.

An opinion born so fast is born prematurely.
Sleep on it or at least when asked for one,
look into nothingness and quietly blink on it.
You may know what you think or
you may want to know more,
Don't fall for others' opinions,
There are enough tic-tac-toe lifers,
don't you go make one more,
or not, and that's really all there is to it.

Jerks and Tears

No man can stand a wave of men
without men behind him
it is true of a woman too, dare I say
that with her, side all of them.

Not all men can starve and watch
their starving mothers beaten,
abused by alcoholic fathers
and not be a wife beater.

Not all men even know that
such behavior can be bettered.

Not all men can be feared and
respected in public eye and
Be respectful before seeking respect
Be a supporter of women before using #feminism
Be not hypothetical or a hypocrite.
Not all men even know that
such men too are mortal.

Not all men can be cajoled, incited
encouraged, enticed, threatened or
commanded to not be jerks.
Not all men who know this are
men who pretend not to know.

Not all men who feel the same
know how to handle shame.
Shame and anger, the latter same
as of outraged women everywhere.
But shame, to be voiced and acted upon
wherever something shrouds the sun
and another human needs some help
and a human alone can pay attention.

Not all men know how to cry for others.
Not all men even know why to.

Not all men are trying to be feminists.
Not all men are even trying to.
Not all men who can change others are trying to.

Until when some men and some women
quietly behind the hashtag wars
do some good together
do some good that lasts
to end this ancient farce
one gets the stick and other gets the carrot
one for the luck and other as the mascot
one is victim and the other, victim by association

Until then,
those tears that women do not deserve,
that are forced from them by jerks;
Those tears that men must learn to shed
Never forget the workings of jerks;
Those tears that are too often shed too late
must not be shed for jerks.
We must tear into their ranks,
and let jerk tears flow

Until then, #NotAllMen is no excuse
it must be a call to arms.
be careful with the taken for granted
with what you think you know

Space Surfers

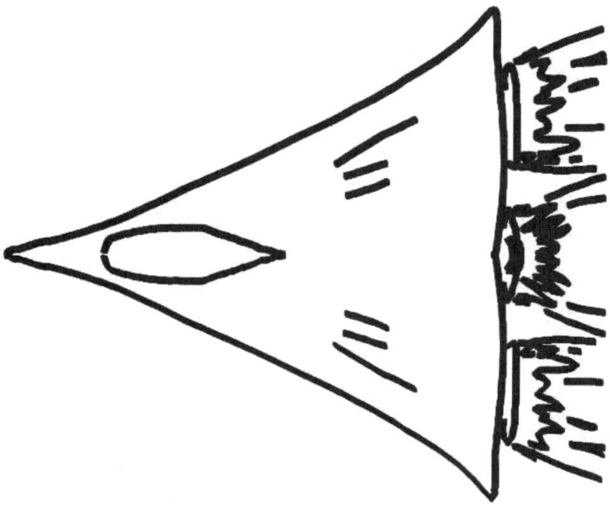

Wisps of smoke drift upwards into the sky
welcomed by moonlight and the stars
Lying close to the fire, she exhales
purple smoke into the thin air
which turns crimson very soon
and she laughs every time it does.

Glittering dust from the bones and stones
whirl about as lazy devils upon white

salt that covers all before glowing blue mountains
Glowing, as if from within, a scary sight.

A party returns to refuel and barter
someone repairs a frailty meter
one man takes off his solar sail wings
and oils his blades from the sparkling springs
while another opens a fizzy drink
that catches fire before it is drunk
She watches all, lazily, burping,
looking at the adventure and lifelessness
all around and sighs. The food is all eaten.
The trip is almost a success.
The record is almost set.
Their hero homecoming guaranteed.

She looks up at the spent red dwarf setting
off in the North beyond the Great Gorges
where she sees flareriders swoop
upon lazy spirals of starry flares
and loop around, dangerously close to
the surface shooting sure lances into the star.
she waits.

Mining for Sublime

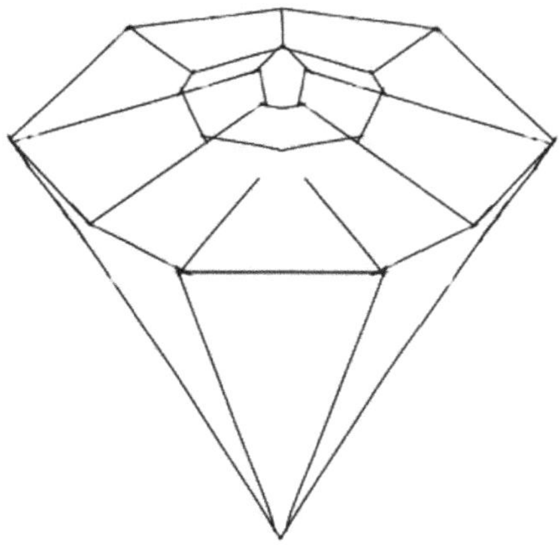

Sometimes these forests of colors blind me,
while I am out walking on autumn evenings.
A crow for company and silence otherwise;
A dying storm of moods in my musings
broken only by cawing at the setting
of the sun beyond the lake.

Colorful leaves, carelessly littered about
the once neat stone paved road
beside the old haveli that housed
long dead princes and their consorts,
will one day rise through the roots

to turn green again,
I won't be here nor will this crow
perhaps these trees will remember.

I don't mind being blinded by the leaves
which returned their green to the tree
before falling, only so they could be broken down.
And then to be mined from under dirt
and raised once again after winter
as the crown of maybe another tree.
From birth till death and rebirth again,
to sing another's life giving refrain.
To become dirt and be mined from under,
to rise up into life and something sublime.

Smoke rises from my chimney
telling me dinner is ready
and the crow caws expectantly,
as is its wont at the end of autumn days
when dusk calls me out for walks
down by the lake, beside the forests
only to retire to a mountain song
and burnt chicken, whose bones we share
just in time to watch the stars come alive
and then we are quiet.
The night is good but we have sunlight to miss
even if it sometimes blinds me with its colors
even if we know that it is coming
we cannot wait for our autumn day to be reborn.

Lake of Faults

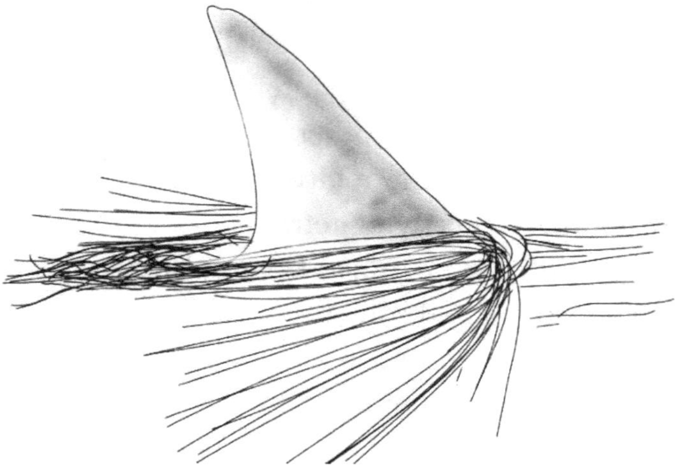

Six sided crystal magic from the clouds
blankets all with its powdery fragility
blinds all with its glow and hides the track
that winds up the Himalayan valley

Many have made this one way trek
ending in a red shower on the white
in the valley below.
Many unceremoniously dragged

to a bloodless death amidst life
in the lake above.

Life here is only a figure of speech
buried in the bones of those long gone
and those who are now undead there,
their last emotions etched forever
in leathery skin and yellowing teeth.

Waiting for Execution

Tap drips below the mirror
where long stares see vanishing hair,
sunken eyes, stubbled cheeks
brow lines and fat chin of despair.

Thoughts swirl as mindless clicks
separated by playing paper toss
aiming at and missing the bin
the usual trudging to and fro the gym
the rationalization of any loss
the unfounded belief in another day
another task, another project with
another manager and a little more say

Today is a snapshot of stairs,
winding, going up or down
or going and coming back around.
Destination, remuneration, progression,
decided in secret affairs

Today is hope reanimated by sunk cost.
Time that once was free of cost,
Time that was technically overtime.
Time that was practically lost,
Time that nobody in particular valued
any more than a life indentured.
Time that a family and dreams needed
more than the tricks the monkey learned.
Time that was a hope for a different outcome
while doing nothing different and going home.
Today is hope, joined to reality with a rope
maybe hanging on, maybe already hanged.

Now is the time when faint clock ticks
impossible to hear over conference calls,
loud anecdotes and sharp inquiries,
are heard.
Now, when the rules are set, the program is on,
the progress bar is filling up. A tiny window of hope
opens while you wait for execution.

Where War We

Where prim prose prods primed primates
to purge pure evil from enemies.
Radicals release repressed reveries
rousing raves rarely reprieved;
Roaring repulsed reviews
received rudely by the depraved
There we war.

Where ambitious aim for autonomy
from assured anarchy by automation.
Where omnipotent overlords overrule
outrageous orders from the ordinary.
Where stoic successors scram suddenly
subject to sure missives from messiah.
Where powerful pursue purulent purpose
prizing prized possessions from poverty.
Where lamenting laughable laws lands
laymen in locked up rooms without loos.
Where rhetoric ruins rationality
truly revels in raping true liberty;
Negates the nature of nationality
parading hack history as patriotic duty;
There war we.

Price of Freedom

One day the man Jerry, tired and forlorn
slumps into his sofa with his phone
In a while, Maggie will be back with groceries
it will be time to cook, and talk and moan

In a while, the gap of work and life
will have been bridged by some alone time
Switching off the lights and the screens
the man knocks back on the sofa
eyes closed but his phone pings

some goof with a comic cartoon
some colleague with a silver spoon
some uncle with his urgent forward
some stud with exclusive scheme
some aunty with random scheme
some childhood friend with uncomfortable familiarity
some unknown number with disguised hilarity
some company with unwelcome ads
some others with stuff free of charge
some grabbers of your peace of mind
some satisfied with just eyeballs
No one with any regard for the time
the priceless seconds of slumping on the sofa
before life restarts.

The bell rings.
No it's his phone that pings.
No it is a dream perhaps
filled with chiming bells, whistles and rings
No it is the bell, urgent in calling.
getting up to open to door to a scolding
for napping, for not offering
to take even one of the bags she's carrying

After tucking in the produce in the fridge
and the wife in the bubble bath

he wears his apron and sharpens his blade.
He cuts the meat. Now, wide awake.

Lost in the rhythm he listens to music
in his head, he is slicing up the tension,
grating all confusion, dicing up build up,
prepping for rejuvenation.
His phone pings from his sofa. He does not hear.

He feels hands slide up from behind him.
Soft hands grasping at him, as he laughs
softly caressing his stubble and cheeks.
He lays the knife down reaching for her behind.
She steps backs, leaning forward eluding
his touch, squirming, as he laughs.
One hand holds the back of his head,
while the other slides around his neck.
He hears his phone ping behind him
as she chloroforms him to the floor.

He feels his hands numb and cold.
He opens his eyes to find himself outdoors.
Cold and dressed in new clothes.
He is on a chair outside a door.
It is familiar. Maybe… Yes, it is his own door.
He rings the bell. He tries the door.
It is open. He walks in to a dark room.

The light for the walkway isn't working.
He shuffles on to the hall and reaches to his right.
Click!
"Surprise!!!"
A gaggle of smiling faces greet him.
"Happy Birthday Mike!"
All of that evening, Mike/Jerry shakes hands,
smiles at selfies, cuts his photo cake,
makes his wishes, chief among which
is that the fear that Maggie knows everything
be unfounded. if price of his freedom
is only his birthday, he is ok.

The Princess of Flies

The princess sat beside her father
at the feast of the smiling dogs
hearing the bard sing of days long
hidden in illogical songs

On her left the balcony looked
over the maze in the garden

She longed to run through the maze and
reach beyond for woodland eden

That boy could be right, the son of the knight
who was afraid of riding, but sure of what was right
He told her of seedy pubs along dingy roads
and mauling cutthroats on lonely crossroads
and reeking towns of filth, soldiers and broads
where lovely pink maidens meet bloody red swords
in an effort to see some form of fright

Though the princess yearned for free air
in its absence, as is now, to be freer
She wanted most of all to run through her garden
To see the river in her eden that she can hear
She craved.

About the Author

Purujeet Parida was born in Odisha where he went to school and fell in love with Nature, Languages and Indian Culture. Quiet and introspective by nature, he grew up tinkering with his fiction books, paintbrushes and Violin. Naturally, after school he went to study engineering. After completing his engineering degree, he went to Mumbai to work for an Investment bank in 2011. While he has been writing poems since childhood, Office life in Mumbai provided the blender of perspectives and prejudices that inspired this collection of poems.

Apart from Writing, Purujeet is passionate about traveling and star gazing – of the astronomical, not the Bollywood variety. He also regularly cooks Indian and continental cuisine for friends and family and has never caused anyone to visit the doctor. Being an avid carnivore, his love of cooking barely compares to his love for eating all kinds of food – especially the bizarre kind. He is fluent in five languages and is learning two new languages presently.

He can be contacted by mail and even be enticed to meeting strangers over cups of coffee and promises of healthy discussions over any topic under the sun.

You can check out more about Purujeet and his activities at the links provided below.

Site: about.me/Purujeet

Blog: sfscient.wordpress.com

Mail: mailpurujeet@gmail.com